A Solitary woman

Tanka by
Pamela A. Babusci

Susan,
enjoy...
love & light
[signature]

Y5/14

Introduction by David Terelinck
Cover Art by Larry DeKock

"Painting is poetry that is seen rather than felt, and poetry is painting that is felt rather than seen."

—Leonardo da Vinci

I wish to thank my good friend, artist Larry DeKock for the use of his beautiful oil painting, *Still Water Bath,* to grace the cover of my tanka book. Larry and I have collaborated at several art galleries in Rochester, NY; I have written tanka to accompany his exquisite paintings.

A heartfelt and warm thank you to Luminita Suse who helped me tremendously with the cover art layout and design. She was an angel to assist me with many long hours of her hard work and patience.

My deep gratitude to David Terelinck for writing his wonderful introduction.

To Leza Lowitz and Claire Everett for their exquisite book blurbs, I give my sincere gratitude.

Christina Nyguen and Mary Lou Bittle-DeLapa, many thanks for proof-reading and making suggestions to my manuscript.

Without my seamless fabric of good friends, *A Solitary Woman* would never have been published. I am most grateful and blessed to have all these amazing and talented people in my life.

Pamela A. Babusci

Introduction

A Solitary Woman always has a story to share, and Pamela A. Babusci shows this to us in a unique and refreshing manner. When I read the poems within *A Solitary Woman*, I was reminded of the words of Virginia Woolf, for Pamela is no ordinary poet, but someone who writes *"not with the fingers, but with the whole person."* In her carefully crafted poems we feel *"the nerve which controls the pen wind itself about every fibre of our being."* We sense ourselves being stitched into every poem as she *"threads the heart"* and pierces our soul with offerings of the most personal parts of her life.

The tanka within *A Solitary Woman* are infused with the life-blood of the poet and mirror the joys, loves and losses within her life. The title tanka is rich with the symbolism of a woman who has loved much, lost love, and yet still has so much to give:

a solitary woman
knows a heartache
or two
tossing scarlet petals
into her evening bath

Despite the heartache that has coloured her life, this woman does not shy away from sensuality and passion, or the ritual of invoking love, of self and others. These scarlet petals may well be memories of old lovers and good times, or incantations for ones yet to arrive.

Pamela treats this short poetry form with all the respect a thirteen-hundred year history demands. In her skilfully written poems there is homage to the style, form and content of female tanka masters from the courtly age. Her poems are serious studies of life and all the emotions it can encompass. She has the ability to capture a moment as simple as a tea ceremony, but in a way that is suggestive of the quietus our personal lives.

warm rain
spilling down bamboo
the stillness
of green tea
before the whisk

This poet is not afraid to use contemporary innovation within style and structure if it is in the best interest of the poem. For all the phonic brevity in the following tanka there is no loss of rhythm, lyricism and meaning. The very short lines create a tanka of sensual urgency that rides the boundaries of being openly sexy. Through this structure Pamela gives us an undercurrent of sexual tension every bit as powerful as the static charge in the ozone before the lightning bolt cracks:

heat lightning—
the long
run
in my
silk stockings

Pamela's writing gives her tanka a tangibility that might otherwise be lost with a less gifted poet. In her hands we can smell the very essence of a relationship, be it good or bad:

cherry blossom tattoo
the scent traveling
up my arm
after all these years
this permanent stain of you

We can see the iridescence of the moon on skin and feel the faint edge of remodeled collagen as a finger traces assaults from the past:

pure moonlight—
three years post cancer
the long surgical scar
fading into the belly
of my womanhood

The softness of feminine skin should not be confused with weakness. In this collection we see a passionate woman who has survived cancer, betrayal, abandonment, despair, the death of family members, and a broken heart. In spite of this there is a dignity in her acceptance of that which cannot be changed. An understanding of the gifts that are to be found in her aloneness, and in her recognition of her place in the universe:

autumn of my life
motherless, fatherless
childless
i gather citron stars
tether them to my heart

a woman's destiny
is not always
within her power
tonight, all the stars
are her unborn children

These poems are not based on adolescent concepts of romantic dreams of love. Rather they are grounded in the fidelity of someone who has "been there" and thus give rise to an honest collection that will be appreciated by the mature reader. There is credibility in this writing and the tanka are fresh and uncontrived. The following tanka is a personal favourite as, like Pamela, I have watched my own parents perform the very same waltz many times.

this morning dance
of who's right
who's wrong
i remember mother always
letting my father lead

However, the poet's relationship with her mother was not a happy one. It was strained and emotionally distant. Abuse does not always have to come at the end of a hand or fist, but can be found in silent and dismissive acts, and the rationing of love:

her love was voiceless——
finding a note i gave
my mother
when I was eight
hidden in her prayer book

And when these words do come, they can be painful, sharp and every bit as damaging as silence:

my mother
did she realize the power
of her words?
beneath snowy pines
forgiveness begins

The cathartic process of committing these tanka to paper allows Pamela to continue her healing journey in respect of her parental relationships. There is a gentle poignancy in the realization that any future healing can only happen with the distance that death brings:

autumn has taken on
a deeper shade of
crimson this year
missing my parents more
with each falling leaf

Within these poems, *A Solitary Woman* speaks with a strong voice without a trace of hubris or self-consciousness. In sharing scenes from the chaos of love, loss and betrayal, there is a rising awareness that this woman is not a victim. The tanka are not self-indulgent, but a means of remediating the hurts of the past and moving forward in life through honest expression:

biting into
a ripe pomegranate
it was you
who cheated
not me

giving
back the ring
taking
back my heart
April rain

confetti stars
across the Milky Way
i had my reasons
for leaving
his for begging

The influence of Pamela's role as editor of *Moonbathing: a journal of women's tanka* is evident in this collection. The poems within *A Solitary Woman* are a celebration of femaleness and the journey to acceptance of this place in life.

She uses her tanka to construct a mosaic of the landscape many women walk through in life. Pamela paints stories of love and loss, lack of motherhood and barrenness, joy and despair. And she portrays this solitary woman as one of enduring strength who walks lightly upon the earth with compassion and sensitivity for those around her. A woman who, undoubtedly, will survive.

leave me alone
with autumn winds
& these falling leaves
tomorrow i will heal
my shattered heart

learning a heart
can survive
many breaks
i pluck bloodroot
to stain my soul

When *A Solitary Woman* comes into your life, her
story will be one that will touches you personally and
makes you feel that your whole being is involved. Like
'borrowed moonlight' she will leave a timeless mark
upon your soul and unfailingly deepen your
awareness of the feminine heart.

David Terelinck, Australia
Author of *Casting Shadows: collected tanka*

snowed in
we drink
more than
dirty
martinis

in your hands
i become a pebble
polished smooth
hot petals fall
from your lips to mine

memorizing your face
every detail
every curve
tracing your birthmark
with my tongue

too shy to reveal
my hidden passions & yet
i dream about you
taking refuge within
my supple breasts

confetti stars
across the Milky Way
i had my reasons
for leaving
his for begging

you stand before me
like Cezanne's still life
painting
silent & motionless
no apology given

you already possess
these vermilion lips
what more do you need
what more do you want
my foolish lover?

sky-gazing
the fire-red streaks
of shooting stars
our passion burns out
like a meteor shower

spider mum
weave your liquid petals
around
the tendrils of our passion
& the whiteness of love

a solitary woman
knows a heartache
or two
tossing scarlet petals
into her evening bath

my thirst
for you can never be
quenched
soft rain on hyacinths
stain our leafless bodies

when i think i know
everything about love
i fall in love
for the
first time

you have given me
diamonds pearls
& lavish flowers
still a piece of your heart
that's inaccessible

life sometimes
gets too
overwhelming
that i just want a man
to rain upon me

blood-red stilettos
the power i feel in them
the power
i surrender
when removed

new year's eve
how soundlessly snowflakes
fall into tomorrow
i awaken inside a white cocoon
of loneliness

folding up
her heart into a neat
origami box
careful not to spill
out the brokenness

putting a brush
into paint & paint
onto canvas
i express my feelings
in variations of blue

learning a heart
can survive
many breaks
i pluck bloodroot
to stain my soul

i am in a funk
turquoise, sapphire, indigo
azure & cobalt
out of my skin
out of my bones blue

who knows
how to live with
heartache?
finishing my self-portrait
with layers of regret

i am sorry
i broke your heart
but, what about mine?
we are all living
fiery star to fiery star

leave me alone
with autumn winds
& these falling leaves
tomorrow i will heal
my shattered heart

at night
she sheds her veneers
& escapes
into a blue river
of morning glories

cutting
turquoise-blue hyacinths
the color of sky
i visit my sister
who just miscarried

drawing bath water
tepid not hot
i hate
that i still
love you

the green wind
of a summer evening
how it parts
the sadness
of a dying lotus

i want to sleep
in a field of wild poppies
let their
red flesh envelop me
& my broken heart

a van Gogh
starry night
i load
my paintbrush with his
torment & despair

as you undress me
you can never remove
all my childhood wounds
i keep hidden
even from myself

starless sky
i stir the windchimes
to convince myself
i am not alone
in this vast universe

how vulnerable
the woman in Picasso's
Blue Nude
sitting with despair
& the weight of the world

how beautiful
my mother's silhouette
against the spring window
finding out she was
pregnant with me

six years old
always trying to please
my mother
by being the
surrogate mom

transforming
her former self
into her new self
looking into the mirror
she sees her mother

carrying secrets
from one generation
to the next
i find my mother's diary
and burn it

her love was voiceless—
finding a note i gave
my mother
when i was eight
hidden in her prayer book

ageless mountain—
putting
our mother
into a
nursing home

drinking black coffee
my heart stained
by bitter words
why did my mother stay
in an unhappy marriage?

this morning dance
of who's right
who's wrong
i remember mother always
letting my father lead

after
my mother's funeral
i vanish
into the mirror
removing all my make-up

never living up
to mother's
expectations
now, i visit her grave
in silence

pure red
the saturated color
of a broken heart
i plant wildflowers
on my mother's grave

with blue irises
a woman in white
carries sorrow
down a path
nobody wants to go

autumn rain—
sorting through
my dead
mother's
photos

planting a tree
in my mother's name
why when she was alive
unable
to hug me?

growing up
i felt invisible
my mother
did she know
the depth of my love?

i cannot separate
my feelings of love
from hate
mother on the horizon
in her flowing white gown

my mother
did she realize the power
of her words?
beneath snowy pines
forgiveness begins

prayers
for inner-healing
thoughts of mother's
abuse
thinning in the mist

a black butterfly
lands on the white sea
of her dreams
sometimes a heart
can drown in grief

first calligraphy
the feel of it
on rice paper
writing a love letter
to my deceased mother

first winter dream
i float inside the heart
of my mother's womb
evening snow blankets
my innocent body

this is
no ordinary prayer
that moves me to tears
anniversary
of my mother's death

making grandmother's
cassata cake
i ponder the beauty
of her Sicilian eyes
& the hills of her village

never learning Italian
because my parents
were discriminated against
now, i listen to
Puccini & weep

even at 84
how caustic
my father's words
my therapist's number
disconnected

all the
wildflowers have gone
to seed
my father has returned
to the earth

after father's death
my sisters & i
clean out
all the shattered pieces
of our dysfunctional family

resurrecting & reading
my parents' love letters
for the first time
i accept
their relationship

autumn has taken on
a deeper shade of crimson
this year
missing my parents more
with each falling leaf

visiting
her lover's grave—
a dying chrysanthemum
casts its shadow
upon her heart

who will cast
the longest shadows
upon my grave
naked willow branches,
unkempt hair of mourners?

will i be remembered
as a poet
a lover or a fool?
wild asters flooding
in autumn rains

all my life
a barren womb—
pregnant spring
giving birth to nameless
& numberless flowers

never pregnant
i cut into a ripe
pomegranate
red seeds flowing
down the barren sink

autumn of my life
motherless, fatherless
childless
i gather citron stars
tether them to my heart

a woman's destiny
is not always
within her power
tonight, all the stars
are her unborn children

motley autumn leaves
start to fall into
my heart's void
middle aged
& childless

pregnant spring
everywhere the scent
of new life
the lingering pain
of being childless

deep inside the core
of O'Keeffe's *Red Canna*
is a fiery river
flowing into the canyon
of every woman

betrayed by a friend
is worse
than by a lover
there are secrets
a lover doesn't know

i walk for miles
after your betrayal
my black beret
white and heavy
in the falling snow

i arrive home
with the autumn wind
in my hair
is it too late to ask
for forgiveness?

i carry
borrowed moonlight
into the house
only a translucent memory
of myself exists

a heart
devoid of love
is an empty vessel
after praying to Buddha
his deep silence

the coolness of your lips—
you cannot hide
your fading passion
i cannot look into
your cheating eyes

i can relate
to you
Sylvia Plath
how your jilted heart
still hangs on the elm

after the affair
she rides a blue moonbeam
straight into
the poverty
of his heart

he leaves
this morning
without touching her
between sips of java
a bitter taste

standing on the pier
of my life
should i jump in
should i let the ocean
fill me with indigo dreams?

copious rain
i stare out the window
and get lost in
the fluid essence
of missing you

i visualize
Chagall's indigo paint
washing over
his *Blue Lovers*
in one continuous stroke

you embrace me
as if we'll never
embrace again
the moon slowly sets
on a field of poppies

praying to Buddha
in solitude
i feel weightless
like falling snow
under the Milky Way

centering prayer
again
i am enfolded
in a love
beyond my comprehension

questioning
God's existence
i throw my rosary
against the bedroom wall
without guilt

feeling guilty
for the harsh words
i spoke in anger
the rest of the day
i spend in silence

his love
is like an opiate
she craves
lying in a field
of blood-shot poppies

white mist rising
around the pond
i seek out
blue lotus perfume
clinging to your nakedness

he tattooed
his heart into hers
slowly
a crimson hibiscus opens
scattering pollen

cherry blossom tattoo
the scent traveling
up my arm
after all these years
this permanent stain of you

after
the break-up
she comes home
with a deep-red
dragon tattoo

this body permanently
stained by yours
like pollen
from a floating lotus
embedded in my heart

skinny dipping
in a summer river
a million stars
clothe us
in liquid light

you altered my body
to fit into yours—
how gracefully
the paper-whites bend
towards the moon

the intense white
of chrysanthemums
while making love
i become
a thousand petals

swimming
towards the white light
she awakens
to four blue walls
in the recovery room

a diagnosis
of ovarian cancer
suddenly
plum petals fall
outside my hospital window

in my dream
running scared
through a wildflower field
this morning is the first day
of chemo

after chemo
getting thinner & thinner
my body
its shadow
fading on the wall

hair falling out
in clumps in my brush
on the floor
like petals
of a dying lotus

who will rebuild
the ruins of my heart
after cancer?
i scoop up liquid stars
& drink them

never thought
i'd be a cancer patient
& a survivor
the miracle
of falling snow

pure moonlight—
three years post cancer
the long surgical scar
fading into the belly
of my womanhood

i am just a two-year old
trapped in a woman's body
losing you
to another
lover

53

i refuse to give into
these ebony clouds
isn't it enough to realize
that you will
never return?

it's over & then you
kiss me
that kiss
that transcends
all unforgiveness

biting into
a ripe pomegranate
it was you
who cheated
not me

suddenly i want
to take flight into
your inaccessible heart
tear it open
watch it ooze

losing herself
within these stark white walls
disappearing
unnoticed
a shell of a woman

heat lightning
penetrates
the garnet sky
let me travel the flesh
that borders your lips

what gives me
more ecstasy
a calla lily opening
or your fingers
exploring me?

giving
back the ring
taking
back my heart
April rain

like a wounded
soldier looking
to stop the pain
i too seek refuge
in this stranger's arms

crushing
white lotus roots
into pulp
the more i gave
the more he wanted

naked willow branches
ripple the stream
i cross
the mist covered bridge
into tomorrow

suspended moon
i hang onto
every word
he hasn't
spoken

no sleep
for the jilted lover
the incessant drip
of lingerie
gives her a migraine

how translucent
the heart
of this pink waterlily
& yours walled off
like steel petals

new year's eve
looking for love
in the personals
no comfort in reading
the psalms

rejected lover
she sucks
all the marrow
from the
bones

her dimly lit heart
resembles fireflies
dying
she changes the vase water
& adds fresh flowers

river of stars
in the pond
i scoop up
Orion's belt & tie it
around my heart

a single hyacinth
perfumes the paper screen
i could linger
a thousand
summers

how many times
have we broken
the same promise?
you sleep on the couch
i read Plath's journal

Saturday night
cleaning out
the closets
full of his clothes
& emotional baggage

from a hot shower
i rise out
like white mist
into the arms
of a new day

wrapping herself
in a dragon kimono
her spirit
flies off like a kite
with an eternal string

yellow lotus
mirrored in the autumn pond
enclosed
within each petal
the stillness of saffron

what is life
without love?
without passion?
i inhale whiteness
i exhale blueness

surrendering
to life & its journey
is not easy
a milkweed seed adrift
on colorless wind

you never ask
if i still love you
silent
during lovemaking
silent, my tears

gazing at a field of
wild crimson poppies
all their fire
ignites a passion in me
i thought was dead

bleaching
scarlet flowers
white
how many times must i say
i am sorry?

the pearl growing
inside my heart
opaque like
endless stars
light years away

in the terra-cotta pot
tumbling pear blossoms
when will i be free
from him
free from his words?

beneath the weight
of his body or next to
a stand of pines
i am quite small
& yet & yet

how do i cure
this deep-seated love?
you've moved on
& i stand in the pouring rain
without an umbrella

warm rain
spilling down bamboo
the stillness
of green tea
before the whisk

sixty springs
have come & sixty springs
have gone
i am still looking for that
perfect plum blossom

morning fog
through a poppy field
scent of crimson
on my hands
as i pick summer

springtime passed
& still no lover
combing
my hair
a thousand times

Milky Way swirling
in martini glasses
with each sip
we swallow
star after star

as if seeing love
for the first time
you bring me
white peonies
wet with morning dew

her porcelain skin
newly washed like
a fresh water pearl
she awaits her lover's footprints
across the dewy path

Acknowledgements

A Hundred Gourds, American Tanka, Eucalypt, Gusts, Magnapoets, Notes from the Gean, Ribbons, Ribbons Newsletter, Saigyo Tanka Contest First Place Award, Love Tanka Contest Honorable Mention, The 6th International Japan Tanka Contest Certificate of Merit Award, The 7th International Japan Tanka Contest Excellence Award, Inaugural Tanka Way Contest First Place Award, Modern English Tanka, red lights, Skylark, Ash Moon Anthology, Lynx, Poetry Portal, Haiga-on-line, Kokako, Raw NerVZ Haiku, moonset, tangled hair, kernels, Many Windows Anthology, still: dew-on-line, Butterfly Away Anthology, Haiku Pix Review, Simply Haiku, Lakeview, 3 Lights Gallery, Blithe Spirit, multiverses, Wisteria, The Temple Bell Stops Anthology, c22 anthology, Petrichor: Anthology of Short Verse, A Woman's Health Magazine, Ink Sweat & Tears, Breast Cancer Coalition Newsletter, Wisteria, Eroticism in Art & Literature, Princess Haiku, Take Five: Best of Contemporary Tanka, Fire Pearls: Short Masterpieces of the Human Heart.

About the Poet

Pamela A. Babusci is an internationally award-winning haiku/tanka & haiga artist. Some of her awards include: Museum of Haiku Literature Award, International Tanka Splendor Awards, First Place Tanka Yellow Moon Competition (Aust), First Place Kokako Tanka Competition (NZ), First Place Saigyo Tanka Competition (US), First Place Inaugural Tanka Festival, 6th International Japan Tanka Contest Certificate of Merit Award, The 7th International Japan Tanka Contest Excellence Award.

She has illustrated several books, including *Full Moon Tide: The Best of Tanka Splendor Awards*, *Taboo Haiku*, *Take Five: Best Contemporary Tanka Vol.1*, *The Delicate Dance of Wings*, *Chasing the Sun: selected haiku from HNA 2007 and* was also the logo artist for Haiku North America in NYC in 2003 and HNA in Winston-Salem, NC in 2007.

Pamela A. Babusci is the founder and the editor of: *Moonbathing: a journal of women's tanka*, the first all-women's international tanka journal.

Poetry and art have been an integral part of her existence since her early teenage years. She has a deep desire to be creative on a daily basis. It feeds her spirit and soul, gives meaning to her life, and will continue to be a driving force until she meets her creator.

76

Made in the USA
Charleston, SC
22 December 2013